GW00836238

How to
Teach the
Mentally Retarded—
There's a Way to Reach Them

Gloria H. Hawley

VICTOR
BOOKS a division of SP Publications, Inc.
WHEATON, ILLINOIS 60187

Offices also in
Whitby, Ontario, Canada
Amersham-on-the-Hill, Bucks, England

Fifth printing, 1983

Scripture quotations are from the King James Version, and the *New American Standard Bible* (NASB), © 1960, 1962, 1963, 1968, 1971, 1972, 1973 by the Lockman Foundation, La Habra, California. Used by permission.
ISBN: 0-88207-180-7

VICTOR BOOKS
A division of SP Publications
P.O. Box 1825 • Wheaton, Ill.

This book is dedicated
to
Laura and Craig.
They are the teachers.

Contents

Prologue

Numbers, statistics, medical terminology, and volumes enriched by multisyllabic words do not motivate the average lay person to be involved with retarded individuals! Our churches are inundated with programs for every imaginable outreach—except to the mentally disabled.

Perhaps one reason is because mental retardation is a negative label. People are frightened, embarrassed, or repulsed by a crippled intellect, whereas a bright-eyed tot in a wheelchair may stir sympathy and involvement. But a child who stumbles in speech and thought—who grapples with the basic needs of life? A child whose very sensory responses to his environment give him a distorted view of his surroundings?

A retarded child is bound by his infirmity as rigidly as the youngster with a physical infirmity is bound by braces or by a wheelchair. And quite often, in both cases, the impairment lies in the same area of the brain.

Diagnosis and prognosis are not of prime interest to the Sunday School staff. The IQ should not be the focus. The *individual* is important! Learning to know the *person* should come first, and then the gleaning of additional information through books.

There are no typical people who represent all retarded individuals. Conditions overlap. Behavior defies charts. Learning ability transcends stereotypes.

The church is not a clinic, nor should its classes compete on the same level as Special Education classes in the schools. Sunday School presents the Gospel of Jesus Christ. The Sunday School teacher presents the love and the Person of Jesus Christ, and the Holy Spirit teaches, informs, instructs, and ministers.

This book proposes to communicate the humanity, dignity, and worth of the mentally retarded. It has been written to remove myth, mystery, and stigma; and to stir readers to open the doors of their hearts and of their churches to these "least" ones for whom Christ died.

This book was requested by Scripture Press Publications to complement their Bible curriculum for the mentally handicapped. As I write, I am unable to view the retarded from an ivory tower of disassociation. Retarded people and their families are a part of my life-style!

Most of the descriptions of Special Education Sunday School classes come from my first-hand experience as the Director of Special Education in my Southern California church.

My beloved children, Laura and Craig, are mentally disabled individuals. Laura, now a quiet, beautiful girl of 20, is classified as "trainable mentally retarded." Craig, an energetic and verbal 12-year-old, is a "multihandicapped" youngster.

As I perused resource volumes and read educational and medical reports to research this book, I did not see my bright-eyed, responsive children in the statistical charts and academic descriptions of characteristics. I did not recognize anyone I knew within the confines of learning limitations or definitions of various diagnoses.

I weary of charts, tables, and learned nomenclature! The average lay church member, willing to help and motivated by the love of Christ, gets lost in the maze of professional superfluity.

This book has been prayerfully designed to encourage you to visualize the retarded individual as a unique human being personally designed and beloved by God.

Take a look—a look deep into his eyes, and see the depths of another soul.

Take a look, and really *see!*

My lovely children have taught me many lessons which will help you see retarded people with new comprehension and appreciation.

We have lived through lessons of pain and patience and play. Lessons of tears and lessons of laughter. Our home encompasses uproar balanced by peace. We have learned discipline together. I have been taught lessons in honesty, dignity, integrity, and forgiveness. The deepest, ongoing lessons are of love, and of courage.

My dearest children.

Retarded children.

God's gift and my teachers.

1 | The Special Child
—Walking in His Shoes

The boy awoke slowly and cautiously. During his seven years of life he had learned to test his responses to his environment. Trial and error—and punishment—had taught him to try to please Mother by "acting right." But so often he was "wrong," and her swift anger sent him into a muddle of fear and confusion. He dimly perceived that he was different. The principle of cause and effect was unknown to him, but he lived with rejection, because of his "difference"—his slowness. Slow of speech and thought. Slow of action and reaction. Slow to learn. Slow to function. But eager to love and be loved! Something within him stirred and yearned for warmth and approval. To belong! Maybe it would happen today.

The little boy gradually became aware that he was wet and cold. He lacked the language to express himself; and because of frustration and fear of his mother, he began to cry. He cried a long time. His misery was compounded by his growing hunger.

When his mother did come to the dark corner where she allowed him to sleep, she began to rage at the youngster because of the odor of his bedding. "Every morning you stink!" she shrieked. "No wonder I drink too much wine! My whole life is spent cleaning up after you, you worthless brat!" She slapped her weeping son and thrust him out of the door, slamming it behind him. "Run away, you idiot! Run away!" Her own face contorted with pain, anguish, and guilt as she went to the wine cabinet and reached for her anesthetic.

The little boy stumbled along. He was a tattered mistake, a travesty of childhood, an insult to the beauty of God's world. He was a retarded child.

A hurrying group of people engulfed him and somehow he found himself inside a house, in the midst of a crowd of adults. One man was talking. The boy lifted his face to the big stranger as a flower turns to the light.

He moved closer. The Man saw him and smiled. The Man reached down and put the youngster on His lap. The deep golden voice flowed over the boy like sunshine and honey. The attentive audience listened, but the boy was unaware of the words. New sensations were surging up from his innermost being. Transcending the strong arms which held him, and the steady beating of the Man's heart—so near his own—was an explosion of relief, of acceptance, of delight, and of love!

The transforming power of love smiled from the Man's eyes and warmed the boy. The child glowed, and darkness retreated from his mind.

The Man, Jesus, was saying, "Whoever receives one child like this in My name, is receiving Me." [1]

We do not find this event recorded in the Bible. It may not have happened just like this. But two facts are true today.

1. The world contains many retarded children.

2. Jesus loves each one!

Retarded people are flesh-and-blood individuals who live out their lives in 24-hour cycles. They have feelings that can be hurt. They have fears, hopes, laughter, and joy. One difference the retarded exhibit is an unbelievable capacity to love. These people respond to a small amount of affection by giving their total love.

Countless mentally disabled youngsters are capable of learning and of functioning. However, progress comes at a slow and sometimes tedious pace, and it involves much repetition. The gamut of mental handicaps ranges from the child with a learning disability to the profoundly retarded individual who requires total physical care. The dictionary defines "retarded" as "held back, delayed, progress impeded."

Causes of mental retardation include brain deficiencies at birth (genetic deviations, organic brain syndrome) and brain damage suffered at some point after birth. Brain damage can occur at any time of life. A baby's development may be interrupted in its mother's womb or an older person may suffer senility. Malnutrition, drug abuse, trauma, cardiovascular or other diseases, anoxia, metabolic imbalance—all these and more contribute to the ranks of mentally disabled people. A careening auto, a micro-organism, or a ruptured blood vessel prove our fragility.

But every handicapped person is of value to God, and has a soul with an eternal destiny!

There are many ways for persons to become "special"—and God Himself planned them all. All children are prescribed by God, are precious in His sight, and have pertinence and purpose in His plan. However, not all children are born perfect.[2]

Mental retardation defies a simple definition acceptable to sociocultural standards, medical nomenclature, and educational concepts. The controversy blurs attempts to standardize identifying criteria from country to country, culture to culture, and even from state to state.

This book will highlight curriculum for the person who is identified as "trainable mentally retarded." He has an IQ of 30-55, is limited in academic skills, and his training will stress help in self-care, social habits, and adjustment to his environment.[3]

The term "children" used throughout these pages refers to mental development; not the physical body, which may be that of an adult. "Child" and "children" are used simply as common denominators. The terms apply to those persons who will always have the hearts and minds of children, regardless of their chronological age.

Prognoses for these individuals can vary downward from the ability to do simple work and accomplish self-support to a need for a protected environment where the individual receives complete care. School systems and municipal facilities, augmented by state and federal funding, offer a variety of services and systems for these individuals.

Spiritual Instruction

But what about the spiritual status of the mentally retarded person? What is available to nourish, edify, and satisfy his inner person?

The ancient Hebrews were certain that children were dear to God! The Psalms and Proverbs are full of illustrations of the protective pattern of family life—and of the spiritual instruction and counsel given within that structure.

In New Testament times, Jesus displayed the Father's loving interest in children, and the childlike. Jesus Christ took time for children. He used them and their activities as examples. And He admonished adults to care for them! He hugged children and took them on His lap. He blessed them and called them His own.

Jesus did not reserve His love for certain groups of children; nor did He exclude various types of youngsters from His love. The heart and attitudes of a "child" are of prime importance to Him. He presented this principle in all four Gospels. "Don't hinder them or hold them back," He said. "Let them come to Me!"

Jesus provided a model the Christian community would do well to emulate—accept all individuals at their various stages of development and minister to them in appropriate ways.[4]

All children respond to the love of God. They do not respond in life-changing ways to a nonchalant "Smile, God loves you!" Their hearts and lives undergo eternal enrichment when they experience God's love through one of His people.

Special children—the so-called "feebleminded," the "idiots," the "retardates"—know exactly who is phony and who is not. The condescending, those with false love, and the professional good Samaritans need not apply for a ministry to them.

The mentally handicapped need to be loved and taught in the power of the Holy Spirit—not with pity or tearful flutterings—but as by Christ, with His strength, His support, and His determination that they *will have His best.*

God says that He allows men to be physically and mentally afflicted (Ex. 4:11). He describes children as a gift or heritage from the Lord (Ps. 127:3). And He declares that He knows each person and forms all people according to His plan (Ps. 139). In the Book of Daniel God states that the most High does according to His will among the inhabitants of earth (Dan. 2:21.) Who can refute or question Him? Jesus, questioned about a man suffering from congenital blindness, acknowledged that the condition existed as a vehicle for the glory of God.

Every church has a responsibility to these special people created by our sovereign God for His specific purposes.

Who are these people, these special "children," these dear ones for whom the Beloved died? There is no stereotype or "typical textbook picture." People vary, and the retarded vary, too.

They're Individuals

Rather than consult medical dictionaries or statistical charts—let's look at a few individuals.

Joey is eight. He has been described by the teaching staff at his school as "a classic case of Down's Syndrome." He is small for his age, affectionate, happy, and displays the physical evidence of his diagnosis. The teachers went "by the book," and Joey's school days were filled with learning good hygiene, domestic tasks, and social acceptance. A substitute teacher inadvertently mixed Joey in with some children working with language arts and discovered that Joey could read several words. He had learned somehow from the teaching given to other youngsters in his classroom.

Joey is now in an intensive tutorial situation and is soaking up academics like a sponge.

Jon, at 17, is six feet tall and well built. He is loud and boisterous. Occasionally he shrieks and capers in a grotesque manner. When Jon was eight years old he was struck by a hit-

and-run driver. In one moment of crushing destruction he was changed from a bright, precocious youngster, into a child stopped forever by mental retardation. He has been hindered and held back, his mental growth impeded.

Laura looks to be 12 or 13, but she is actually 20. Shy, sweet, affectionate, and trusting, she embodies the characteristics of love as described in 1 Corinthians 13:4-7. Her impairment is the result of medical mismanagement at her birth. She cannot speak, but sings praises to her Shepherd in a clear, high voice.

Three-year-old Jenny has a halo of golden curls, a vocabulary of two dozen words, and is growing increasingly curious about her surroundings. Though she is blonde and blue-eyed, her eyes have an Asiatic slant. She has other physiological characteristics which categorize her as a Down's Syndrome child (previously known as "Mongolism" or "Mongolian Idiot"). Jenny's heart is malformed. According to medical logic she should not have survived beyond her first few months. A real miracle baby, Jenny's young parents refer to her as "God's promise." They see her as a gift of love—a vehicle for God's glory, a part of God's plan.

A lively 12-year-old, Craig is a cute little boy. His large eyes sparkle and his sense of humor matches them. Mischievious, winsome, and verbal, he absolutely insists that people respond to him! Craig's head looks too large for his body. Several of his other physical proportions are awry. His fine motor coordination is poor, and his speech lags behind his years. Craig displays hydrocephalus, or "water on the brain," resulting from a surplus of cerebrospinal fluid which pushed out the soft bones of his infant skull, the pressure causing injury to the brain cells.

The young adult who can support himself, but is prey to all the ills of society because of his gullibility, is also mentally retarded.

These are individuals who should be in *your* Sunday School. Their parents, brothers, and sisters should be in your church, functioning as members of the body of Christ!

Do you see them, or others like them, each Sunday?

Essentially the church is people. All the programming and organization are means to the end of bringing about changes in people.[5] However, people are not "conditions," or "statistics," or "textbook cases." People are individuals with value and worth to God. It is not easy to discern people's real spiritual needs, nor their feelings. Only in a warm, accepting atmosphere does a person feel free to be his real self.[6]

Does your church welcome those who are different? Do you? Or are those who are different merely accepted and tolerated in your midst? Are they there at all? If not, where are they?

Parents of mentally disabled children rarely stride into a new church and announce their needs. They shop for a church with care and discretion, often without the child. Dragging a retarded child from church to church can be a shattering experience for all concerned. Parents learn early that it's easier to attend alone, look around, and determine if there is evidence of a loving outreach toward the disabled. Such parents develop sensitive antennae. And when they find a situation lacking love, they hide their hurt and do not return to that church with their child.

Most families with a retarded child do not attend a church. Their own denomination, or the place of worship convenient to their location, usually does not have a program for special people.

Generally speaking, the church should be ashamed. Existing in the community to bring the Good News of Jesus Christ and God's plan of redemption to every person, it falls short in reaching out to the mentally retarded.

Retarded individuals, and their families, are within most communities. Look into the special schools in your vicinity. Attend the P.T.A. sessions there and talk to the parents. Go to your city hall and ask about the programs for the retarded. Observe a few sessions of any programs in your community for the retarded and get to know the parents. Go to any activities in your area for the retarded, such as the Special

Olympics. Write to the National Association for Retarded Citizens in your area.

Special people are within the sphere of your influence!

Find them.

Befriend them.

Invite them to your church.

Share the Word.

"Prove yourselves doers of that Word—and not merely hearers who delude themselves." [7]

[1] Mark 9:37 (NASB).

[2] Hawley, Gloria H., *Laura's Psalm* (Los Angeles: Action House, 1977), p. 91.

[3] Elmer L. Towns and Roberta L. Groff, *Successful Ministry to the Retarded* (Chicago: Moody Press, 1972), p. 127.

[4] R. E. Clark and R. B. Zuck, *Childhood Education in the Church* (Chicago: Moody Press, 1975), p. 18.

[5] LeBar, Lois, *Focus on People* (Westwood, N.J.: Fleming H. Revell Co., 1968), p. 11.

[6] *Ibid.*, p. 30.

[7] James 1:22 (NASB).

2 | The Parents
—Behind the Smiling Mask

The handsome couple, well dressed and outstandingly attractive, hovered over their young son. He too was well groomed.

The parents' faces displayed distress, although strained smiles flickered politely. The little boy was uneasy and fearful.

An usher was telling them that the church could not accept their retarded child in Sunday School. "The teachers have more than they can handle now," he explained, "and we can't expect them to take on a burden like this."

The "burden like this," whose name was Scott, heard every word. He correctly interpreted every intonation and gesture, and promptly became noisily upset. The usher, with an "I told you so" expression, shrugged—and walked away.

Struggling with his composure, the angry father walked out with his family. That family will have nothing to do with religion, churches, and "Christians" to this day!

This is not an isolated incident. Parents of the handicapped, particularly parents of retarded children, regularly experience rejection. One couple, parents of two multihandicapped youngsters, were shunned by neighbors because, "they must have done something *awful* for God to punish them like that!"

Parents are people. The pretty young girl driving the sports car; the tennis champs at the local club; the tanned woman on the beach; the teacher, doctor, bus driver, preacher, and engineer are all parents of retarded children. Can you tell?

What's behind their mask? How do their daily lives differ from your own?

The hurts these people carry go deep. Care for that disabled youngster weighs heavily on father and mother alike. Father, because of the medical and educational costs. Father, because his son will never be accepted at his alma mater. Father, because the fruit of his loins will always remain a child. Mother, because of the constant repetition of routine. Mother, because the neighborhood lacks understanding. Mother, because of the endless conferences with educational and medical personnel! And always the nagging question: "Are we doing *everything* we can for our child?" The fear of the future and the fatigue of today become an intolerable burden which can divide the home. Other children in the family may develop alarming symptoms of neglect, repressed rivalry, or actual overt hatred for the retarded child.

Some families do achieve a measure of balance. However, different stages of family growth may precipitate more upheavals within the family framework. The birth of another child, financial difficulties, adolescence, progressive medical conditions, or family relocation are but a few factors resulting in family crises. Divorce may occur. Or abuse. Frustration causes friction. Parents may oppose or blame each other. The focus of blame may fall on the child, and he is punished because "it's all his fault anyway."

Twisted love may become hate, and a parent sometimes destroys the child while trying to destroy the handicap.

Love and Acceptance

However, there are some families who are united in love and acceptance. When this happens, it is the presence of Jesus Christ in one or both parents.

And even then,
        the hurt goes deep,
    but instead of a root feeding on bitterness—
        the root is refreshed by
Living Water.

When young parents are told of a defect in their child, they do not immediately give thanks to God. Usually, parental acceptance is a hard-fought, private battle for Christians and non-Christians alike. Clichés, unsolicited advice, and even Bible verses ring hollowly in the ears of anguished parents as they grapple with the reality of an imperfect child. These people need the visible support of friends. They need ears that listen without condemnation, and hearts that love without reservation. They also need intercessory prayer on their behalf; that they may respond to God and align their will with His. This takes time, and during that time they experience agonizing internal conflict.

The birth of a mentally handicapped child often has an effect on the parents' religious faith. "If there is a loving God," they say, "why did He allow this to happen?" [1] Even the grieving Christian parent may blame God.

Parental responses to the child can vary from overprotection to total neglect. Reactions may differ, but the results are usually the same: division, disruption, and discord within the family.

Who does understand? The person who has been through it, wrapped in the blanket of God's love—that's who. Those who have endured this stinging experience are the choicest counselors God can use. [2]

The church needs to provide a ministry for the retarded, not only for the pupils, but to allow their parents to interact in an atmosphere of Christian love. Parent can minister to parent. Much of the advice and counsel available to the parents is secular, sometimes opposing biblical principles.

When a church does have Sunday School classes for the retarded, the entire congregation may be blessed. Students enlighten their teachers in many ways. When a teacher is completely dependent on the Holy Spirit to penetrate the intellectual barrier, and must reduce the essence of Scripture to its simplest form, that teacher receives new sensitivity to spiritual things. Teachers of the mentally retarded in Sunday School classes often report life-changing experiences. [3] And, in some cases, parents can give the pastoral staff new insights into the depths of faith, and love, and suffering.

Churches seeking a ministry to the retarded must include the entire family in their plans and goals. A hurt or defective child represents a hurt family. When the Good News of Jesus Christ is presented to the retarded member, others within the family circle may also hear of salvation. God promises that His Word shall accomplish His will! [4] Your job is to dispense His Word to the retarded in a way they will understand. Then you will also want to share His love with the whole family.

He will do the rest!

---

[1] Monroe, Doris, *A Church Ministry to Retarded Persons*, (Nashville: Convention Press, 1972).

[2] Swindoll, Charles, *For Those Who Hurt,* (Portland: Multnomah Press, 1977).

[3] Hawley, Gloria H., "The Root of the Matter," *Christian Life,* (May 1977), p. 42.

[4] Isaiah 55:11.

3 The Home

—Within These Walls

"Home is the sacred refuge of our life," said the 17th century poet, John Dryden. Other definitions of home include "the abiding place of one's affections," "where one likes to be," and "a restful and congenial place."

All Sunday School teachers should know something of the home life of their pupils, and especially teachers of students in the Special Education Department. Teachers who observe children at home better understand children's needs and personalities, thus averting the tendency of the teaching staff to stereotype individuals.[1]

Mentally retarded persons differ from those with normal intelligence in definite ways. However, even the "experts" vary in specific nomenclature to classify and describe the retarded.

A widely read newspaper carried a front page article headlined, "New Optimism Surfacing on Retardation." [2] The writer explained that research by a professor at Brandeis University had revealed data disproving some prevailing attitudes among authorities on mental retardation. According to the article, the retarded individual can develop capabilities far beyond what have usually been attempted. In an interview, the doctor said, "It previously was believed that certain individuals were not educable. We now know this is no longer true."

Philosophies, medical knowledge, and social attitudes fluctuate with time. God's Word is the unchanging plumb line for mankind—the absolute truth on which to base our lives.

Therefore, the church would be wise to focus on the individuals rather than statistics. The curriculum selected should be based on Scripture and written for the mentally retarded. This should be the basic teaching tool which can be adapted to suit needs and abilities of those in the class.

Many of the pupils' needs originate in the home. Your Special Education pupils will come from a variety of environments: overpermissive, superstrict, well-balanced, functioning, broken, or loving homes. Some pupils will come from homes that offer no sanctuary, or are abusive and neglectful. Some will live in foster homes or residential facilities. The Special Education staff must be aware of what transpires in the lives of their pupils during the week. How the youngsters respond on Sunday morning is largely determined by what influences them and sets their behavior during the week.

The Teacher and the Home

Special Education teachers are pioneers and missionaries! They look beyond the Sunday lesson into the eternal souls of their students. They visit, baby-sit, treat to an outing, befriend the family, and pray daily for the household. They breach invisible walls and recognize unknown factors.

If the pupil comes from residential or institutional situations, the staff needs to keep in contact with the recognized line of authority. For instance, certain legalities must be observed before such a resident can be taken on an outing. And the staff should also know and observe specific visiting procedures. In the case of a broken home, teachers find it helpful to know the pattern of visitation rights for the parent living outside the home. The pupil's record should show the name, address, and phone number of each parent.

Sometimes cases of child abuse have been discovered by observant teachers. Needy families have been directed to public aid departments or caseworkers.

Because of genuine love, acceptance, and intercessory

prayer by teachers, some parents have been reconciled to Christ and to each other, thus establishing a healthy family unit in the church.

Dr. Howard Hendricks, professor and chairman of the Department of Christian Education at Dallas Theological Seminary, believes that the *atmosphere* of the home inculcates truth more effectively than the *words spoken*.[3] He explains that teaching is formal and structured, while talking is informal and situational. Hendricks stresses the necessity for a time of fun and enjoyment in the home. All youngsters are constantly recording what goes on about them. Retarded children and adults (trainable or educable) react to the home atmosphere of "truth." If the "truth" being broadcast at home is that Tommy is an idiot and a burden, and "we wish he were dead," Tommy's self-image is affected negatively. If the "truth" transmits the fact that Joanne is a nothing, she will spend more time alone in her room. What "truth" is being fed into your students' minds? Are they secure in the love of the people with whom they live? Are they a treasured part of the family circle? Can they function as an extension of that family?

Be alert in class for disclosures that will provide a clue to the situation. Role play as well as their response to puppets and dolls can be very revealing.

Beyond Expectations

The home is the key, and the key turns both ways. Bible stories sent home with the retarded person may bring the Lord into the center of family living. Scripture, sung or spoken by the retarded, has a poignant effect on those with whom he lives. Retarded people respond to Jesus as presented in the Bible, and that response is a magnet to others. Essentially, children are responders. Parents are the pacesetters, the givers.[4] Love and health go hand in hand. Dr. Rene Spitz conducted institutional research which proved that without love, even normal, well-cared-for children declined into idiocy. But the opposite is also true. A retarded child may respond beyond expectations when given love.

For example, a family with several children of their own adopted a retarded child. Later, when Down's Syndrome was discovered, the family's physician advised that the child be institutionalized. However, the family delayed such action and continued to keep the child at home. As time passed and the child was surrounded with a barrage of love from this warm, closely knit, Christ-centered family circle, he responded. The child, now a preschooler, is actually ahead of other children in some areas.

Because of love.

Because of Jesus.

Because of people willing to be His channel.

Like ancient Jericho, many home environments are surrounded by impregnable walls; and, like Joshua, you can see the walls collapse as a result of your prayerful faith in the power of God!

To whom and to what do your students go home from Sunday School?

You need to know.

---

[1] *Los Angeles Times*, 5 July 1977, p. 1.

[2] Roy B. Zuck and Robert E. Clark, *Childhood Education in the Church* (Chicago: Moody Press, 1975), p. 55.

[3] Hendricks, Howard G., *Say It with Love* (Wheaton, Il.: Victor Books, 1974), pp. 95-97.

[4] Swindoll, Charles R., *You and Your Child* (Nashville: Thomas Nelson Inc., 1977), pp. 60-62.

4

The Teacher

—Not Me, Lord!

"I'd love to help in the Special Education Sunday School, but I haven't had any training or experience," says a church member. This oft-repeated statement is frequently heard by those in charge of church classes for the retarded.

A college student wrote, "I saw they [the retarded] had a real hunger for love, acceptance, and *to feel needed*. I wanted to reach out to them but felt very inadequate. After becoming involved with the Sunday School class, I soon found that by accepting them for who they were, and becoming involved in their lives, I have seen changes in them as well as myself. My experiences with the mentally handicapped have been humbling and rewarding." [1]

Sunday School teachers aren't superhuman, or even super-Christian! They are people like you. The vital common denominator is that the teacher is *Christ's* person. Born again. Saved. Redeemed. Ransomed. A person who has received Christ! A praying person. A teacher available to, and taught by, the Holy Spirit.

Fear restrains many people from teaching, especially in classes for the retarded. Fear because of *my* imperfection and inadequacy. Fear because of *their* (the pupils') imperfections. Fear of the unknown.

Jesus chose imperfect people to be His disciples when He was on earth. They became teachers.

Teaching demands honesty with ourselves. It takes facing just how short we fall of all we should be. Our love for God depends on facing ourselves, realizing our failures and needs, and trusting God's promise of forgiveness through Jesus. Your importance as a person is based squarely on the fact that God loves you. Then God uses you to communicate His love to others. God can use you as a teacher.[2]

A human soul grows and enlarges because of the presence of the Living Christ. That's what it's all about!

Every human soul responds to Him. The psalmist wrote, "The entrance of Thy words giveth light; it giveth understanding to the simple" (Ps. 119:130).

Seeing an individual as beloved and prescribed by God, with an eternal soul and a need for the comfort of Jesus Christ, will dispel your fear.

Love, patience, hope, and faith are key words for you to remember. When in doubt, be *loving*. Be *positive*. Speak of *Jesus*. Demonstrate *His* confidence.

Repetition is another necessary ingredient in teaching the retarded. The story can be told twice, with varying reinforcement, on two consecutive Sundays. (You may even repeat again with role play and again with puppets.) God will give fruit in His time, and when it comes it will be all the more precious!

Pray for creativity and enthusiasm. Be diligent in your own quiet time and personal walk with the Lord. It is of utmost importance that you do not become bored with the routine—and only the Holy Spirit can keep your attitude fresh and new.

Use praise and positive reinforcement lavishly, but honestly. Instead of saying, "That's a good girl, Laurie!" you may say, "Thank you for putting the crayons away, Laurie. That's very good helping!" Use specific praise for a specific action!

Share in a positive manner with the parents. Don't greet them with negative input. Tell them one good thing about their youngster's morning. "Jill enjoyed the music." "Tim helped with the cleanup time." "Margie smiled and seemed very happy today!" Only if it is absolutely necessary, speak to the parent about a disciplinary or medical problem. (The registration sheet should be so designed as to give this information.) [3]

NAME OF CHURCH—SPECIAL EDUCATION

PUPIL'S NAME _____

NAMES OF PARENTS OR GUARDIANS _____

ADDRESS _____

TELEPHONE _____Neighbor or friend's telephone_____

CHILD'S BIRTHDATE _____

DOCTOR'S NAME AND PHONE _____

SCHOOL _____

MEDICATION _____

SEIZURES _____TYPE AND FREQUENCY_____

PHYSICAL DISABILITIES _____

_____

SPECIAL DIET _____

ALLERGIES TO FOOD OR DRINK _____

ALLERGIES TO PETS OR POLLENS _____

DOES HE RESPOND TO ANIMALS?_____

ARE THERE PETS AT HOME? _____

LIST BROTHERS AND SISTERS AND THEIR AGES _____

_____   _____

_____   _____

DOES THE CHILD HAVE SPECIAL FEARS? _____

_____

IS HE ACCEPTED BY THE PEOPLE IN THE NEIGHBORHOOD?____

_____

DOES HE TEND TO WANDER AWAY?_____

CAN HE SWIM?_____DOES HE LIKE WATER PLAY?_____

_____

Please add any other information that will help us care for your child and make him happy and that will enhance our time together_____

_____

_____

Parents should be encouraged as much as possible. That is part of your ministry!

Home visits and outings should be your responsibility also. From these activities you gain insight, experience, and confidence. You also become a friend of the family, which gives you prayer input.

Keeping Order in the Classroom

Some handicapped children are not disciplined by their parents. Regardless of parental reasoning, order must be kept in the classroom. Parents may rationalize, "He doesn't understand," or "I'd feel too cruel," or "He's too different from my other kids and I don't know how to deal with him." One guideline is to allow only what is acceptable in polite society.

Masturbation, filthy language, inappropriate touching or fondling of others will then be prohibited. Swift isolation of the person and a one-on-one confrontation, explaining, "That is not Sunday School behavior. Do not do that here," should solve any such problem. As a once-a-week teacher, you may not be totally aware of what is permitted or even fostered on these special people. Many school systems instill "normalization" in young retarded adults' daily curriculum. Normalization imposes society's standards. Sexual freedom is part of society today. Parents of the retarded are offered classes in the sexual rights of their children. These rights, parents may be told, include the fulfillment of masturbation, and freedom from pregnancy by contraception for both sexes. Homosexuality now looms on the horizon of society's "norm" as a human "right." How soon before these gentle, childlike, special people will be taught this perverted life-style?

As a teacher and a Christian, you have the responsibility counteract the corruption of society, when you encounter it, by example, with God's Word, and by *prayer*. The retarded student will respond to the fact that Sunday School behavior differs from other patterns in his life. You need not impose a long list of "Thou shalt nots" on him. If he knows you love him, and if the Holy Spirit motivates him through your prayers, the youngster will respond. Firm, consistent, simple, loving but decisive discipline *is* successful. Often, the parent or guardian can be tactfully consulted and a mutual effort made to solve any problem.

Giggling or talking out of turn are tolerable. Exposing one's body, threatening behavior toward others, or self-destructive behavior such as violent temper tantrums cannot be tolerated. Your prayers and the wisdom God can give will help. One church class was in an uproar on a particular Sunday. Several of the teachers held an emergency prayer huddle while others of the staff prayed individually with the most disturbed students. Peace prevailed!

Never forget that it is the Lord Jesus Christ whom you serve, and *He will bring the victory!*

From time to time, grateful parents may express a desire to help in the department. Graciously decline their offers. Parents and other relatives should be worshiping, and serving in other areas. Youngsters often learn more readily from persons other than those closest to them. Parents who demand to be involved may supply the snacks or help with transportation, but absolutely should not be in the classroom.

Parents have fears. They fear rejection for their child. They fear that their youngster will exhibit his or her very worst behavior. They fear for the comfort and security of their child. And they fear gossip about their family and its disabled member.

You, the teacher, can ease parental fears by total acceptance of the youngster, by positive input concerning the youngster, and by absolute discretion within the department. *Never, never* let the behavior or circumstances of the retarded be common knowledge to your acquaintances or members of the church. Your job is to justify the family's trust, and to uphold them prayerfully! That means prayer business is private business. Most of what transpires in Special Education is the business of that department only. Positive and endearing aspects may be shared, but not tidbits of untoward behavior merely to satisfy the curious.

Setting Goals

Determine departmental and class goals. Then also set personal goals for the teachers, students, and families. Each teacher can decide before God what He would have him or her prayerfully implement in each child's life. Samples of general goals are:

1. For each child to feel love and acceptance.
2. For each child to realize that Jesus is his personal and eternal Friend.
3. For each child to function at his highest level.
4. For each child's family to be supported and encouraged in love.

Of course, the lessons in the curriculum will have very specific goals related to the Bible content.

Sample goals for the teacher may include:

1. Regular attendance.
2. Call, write, or phone a child each week.
3. Discover one new thing about a child each week.
4. Baby-sit for a family once during the quarter.
5. Pray daily and specifically for a child and family.

Regular meetings of teaching personnel and staff leaders should include evaluation, which helps to determine further goals. Evaluation is looking back to ascertain if predetermined objectives have been reached, and making plans for future lessons based on this information. Such evaluation keeps the staff people- and need-oriented. Evaluation also promotes growth by revealing areas of strength as well as of weakness. This exercise shows personnel where to focus their energies for profitable class sessions.

Questions the teacher can ask himself should include:

1. Were my lesson aims achieved?
2. Did my early activity provide a meaningful introduction to the Bible story?
3. Did my students feel welcomed and important?
4. What should I have done differently?
5. How are my relationships with my co-workers? Are we a team?

As a result of these evaluations, the teacher may think of several areas which need work. He is then free to determine priorities and set goals. Those goals should be specific and realistic. A plan of action should be prayed over and then set in motion.

Teaching Methods

Teaching may be done one-to-one, in a small group, or as a teaching team. No one can prescribe groupings. You must decide what works best in your situation. The most important thing is the teacher's commitment to the slow but strong relationships that will grow with the students. Do not disappoint or frustrate those fragile tendrils of trust reaching out to you from your pupils. They are designed to bear fruit for eternity!

Men as well as women are necessary on the teaching team. Some of the students may not have a dominant male within the framework of their lives. The older boys and young men especially need the strength and stability provided by the Christian male model. Peer presence is also important. Use play helpers—youngsters with youngsters, teens with teens, and young adults with young adults.

A simple, clear approach is best. What abilities do the teachers have? Who can tell the story with verve and contagious enthusiasm? Who can lead the singing in a manner to encourage pupils to sing? And who among the students can read? Who has a good sense of rhythm? Who can help younger pupils? Everyone should be involved. (In one class, a blind college girl teaches a retarded girl of the same age.)

As a Sunday School teacher of the mentally retarded, you have a multifaceted responsibility. This includes your service before God, your sharing with the pupils and their families, your influence to educate the congregation and to help your church obey Scripture. You also have a responsibility to help your community understand mental retardation.

The repetition of routine, while supportive to your students, may begin to bore you. Don't merely teach a story—*love* it over and over! Look into the minds of the class members and see

God at work. Don't be tempted to let the quiet ones just sit there; involve everyone. Encourage expression. Introduce new words. Let them dare to try new skills. Use the Bible story as the basis for song, handwork, play, and conversation. Always teach the Word of God. Bathe all activities in prayer. Depend on the Holy Spirit.

What about salvation for these people? Can they make a decision to receive Christ? We know that only God can see into the heart.[4] Therefore, we dare not make a judgment even in cases of mental disability. Jesus told people to let the children come to Him, and He blessed them.[5] With this example in mind, demonstrate the reality of Jesus Christ and His eternal presence before your students. Remember, you must know your pupils, and your pupils must trust and relate to you before they can respond sincerely. And their response will be determined by their individual capabilities.

The message of Christ, consistently presented and lived by you, will allow eternal decisions to be made. Some of the youngsters won't be able to convey their decisions, but God knows. Your job is to tell them of Jesus. He will save them. Habitual prayer in which the students express themselves to God can be most revealing! Encourage this practice with your class. It will be most beneficial to *you,* the teacher.

Your fears and need of encouragement, and those of the parents, are dim in comparison to the fears harbored by some of your retarded people. Much of their behavior is motivated by their efforts to compensate for what they lack, and to overcome their fears. Try to know of their specific fears—see registration sheet. Respect the reality of their fears. One teacher noted that a new youngster had an overpowering fear of death. Even though it was Easter, the story did not dwell on the Crucifixion. For that particular girl's benefit, the story told of the triumph of Jesus, and dwelt on His love and concern for her. Weeks later, Christ's death and resurrection were presented to Kim, because she was able to tolerate it by then.

Kim has now asked Jesus into her life, and also shared her new faith with a schoolmate. Miraculous attitude changes and responses have occurred in Kim's life. She is no longer in Special Education at church or in the public school system. She is doing well in regular classes in both places.

Be encouraged, teacher! This is one of God's most exciting and rewarding ministries. And He has called *you* to share it with Him!

¹ Walker, Jerry, "My Experiences with the Mentally Handicapped," California State University.

² Richards, Lawrence O., *YOU the Teacher* (Chicago: Moody Press, 1972), pp. 30-34.

³ Special Education Department, First Evangelical Free Church, Fullerton, California.

⁴ 1 Samuel 16:7.

⁵ Matthew 19:14; Mark 10:14; Luke 18:16.

5 The Class

—Flexibility, Not Chaos

Sharing an exciting ministry with God is one thing, but how do you know you've been called? People don't awaken one morning and say, "I'd like to work hard and pray a lot, so I'll go teach the retarded."

The teaching staff must be recruited from the congregation, which must be motivated to respond! First, by prevailing prayer on the part of those in charge. Then by a presentation of the facts by enthusiastic and knowledgeable members of the team. Audiovisuals, such as sound movies of class sessions or narrated slides, are effective. Keeping the congregation aware of class activities in the newsletter or bulletin encourages widespread interest. Use church bulletin boards with pictures of class members or art by the youngsters. Regularly update information for the congregation to keep them cognizant of their special people.

Teaching candidates should be recruited and oriented to Special Education on a regular basis. In one large church, a three-month teacher-training seminar is repeated twice a year.

The qualifications for teaching will vary from church to church. However, one of the basic requirements should include the status of born-again Christians who are willing to pray.

After an observation and training period, a commitment should be made to serve for one year or more. This length of service is necessary to avoid fracturing relationships with the pupils. One lay director of a church Special Education department invites teaching candidates to observe the classes several times, and to sit in on a staff sharing session. The director and candidate then schedule a meeting where the prospective teacher has the opportunity to decline joining the department. No one should feel obligated to teach! Observation with "no strings attached" is of prime importance because it helps dispel fear of the unknown. Even if the individual is not led to join the department, one more member of the congregation has been oriented to your ministry to the mentally retarded.

Remember, the youngsters are in Special Education because they need just that—a special approach to their Christian education. Because of short attention spans, slow learning processes, and physical and mental manifestations of disability, these people do not fit into the regular Sunday School classes.

The difference may be marked or slight; but the retarded person is usually aware of it and feels more comfortable with his peers. Some parent may bring an educable mentally retarded person to a class you have designed for the trainable individual. What then? Or what if an emotionally disturbed or physically disabled youngster is brought to your facility? The general feeling is not to limit God. Most churches are not large enough to attract 20 or 30 individuals who happen to share duplicate handicaps. Therefore, to plan your class for the handicapped effectively, you must assess the needs of the community beforehand. Obtain information from school districts surrounding the church. Then you will know the number of retarded and disabled in your area. Perhaps an institution or residential school is within your area. Parents of disabled people in the church can give you leads to other sources. Public response to pre-registration publicity in local newspapers can help indicate the trend of applicants. Determine the need and then design your class. Keep one thought in mind—FLEXIBILITY! The months spent in prayer will bring sensitivity to God's will and eliminate rigidity in the minds of the leaders. Flexibility is the name of the game.

A Church in California

A church in California considered having a special Sunday School class. The leaders prayed for nearly a year. They surveyed the community, wrote publicity, and recruited teachers. No limits were set on age, ability, diagnosis, or educational status. Their only restriction was the right to exclude any individual who presented a physical threat to others in the group. (During the years the class has been in operation, this right has never been invoked.)

The geographical area contained such a diverse and varied number of disabled individuals that the student enrollment was left in God's hands. When the facility was ready, He brought in the young people. Textbooks advise against mixing handicaps, but in this instance God's limitless resources were tapped. One-on-one teaching bridged the differences, and the class became a success.

Your class will be different because your community is different. You may group individuals according to their ability, and utilize team teaching. You may have one storyteller, one craft person, and one song leader. Of course you will have individual workers to aid the children in their activities. Your curriculum will aid you in setting up your class.

Scripture Press has published a Special Education Bible Curriculum entitled *Happy-Time Course with Pugwug.* The classtime is well planned and the story guidelines are excellent. But remember, the very best curriculum will not teach a retarded child. The Holy Spirit teaches that retarded child, by means of the curriculum (God's Word), filtered through your life. You must be excited and enthusiastic about what you are teaching, and your relationship with Christ must be constantly growing. It's not enough to *tell* the mentally disabled individual, "God loves you." He must *experience* that love through God's people. Through you, Teacher. You cannot give these people what you do not have. A mind-set of who Christ is and what He has done for you will deliver you from self and liberate you to become a giving person with a fruitful ministry.

The *Happy-Time Course,* as it is used by the Holy Spirit,

serves the students. The Course serves the teacher by causing him to reflect on God's love and power. And it serves the family by providing Gospel seeds to grow within the home. The course is a repetitive celebration of worship conveyed in fun and easy learning techniques. You may support the material with simple songs of pertinent Scripture and conversation that reinforces the lesson. Even playtime should be of eternal value as you instill biblical principles of attitude and behavior in the consciousness of your students. Remember, you are ministering to total individuals—not only to impaired intellects. Jesus knows how and where they live. He can give you insights for your teaching.

Class Environment

The special class setting should be bright and inviting! It should also be very practical: near rest rooms, should be carpeted or at least in part, have room to romp, should be accessible to wheelchairs, and have no dangerous attractions, such as sharp objects in a missionary display.

As the students enter, they should be greeted enthusiastically and individually, and immediately involved in an activity center. You may have two or more such centers, depending on the size of your class. Keep in mind that too many choices confuse the retarded. A worker should be stationed at each center to supervise the activity. Newcomers are enrolled and parental information obtained by the secretary or superintendent. (Never let a new youngster be left in class without sufficient registration. You need to know about him for his protection as well as your own.)

Music is an important part of the class. Retarded people respond to and delight in music. Many with speech problems can sing very clearly, because of the cadence and phrasing within a predictable framework of melody. The singing of Scripture is vital because it commits God's Word easily to memory.

Nature centers in the room stimulate interest in the world around your students. Plants graphically teach of life and growth from God. An aquarium with fish and a collection of shells demonstrate the versatility of the sea and God's marine creatures.

Seasons are important and should be illustrated by a bulletin board display. Each season brings its calendar celebration, and most importantly (to your students, at least), *birthdays.* The current birthday people can be honored by a photographic tribute on the bulletin board, as well as mention in class. Personal identity and acceptance can be reinforced with a student bulletin board containing their choice of display. Audiovisuals are important. You will want to include filmstrips, slides, tapes and records of familiar things, and of the students themselves. Outings can be shared on film and tape.

Positive reinforcement through role play, puppets, and flannelboard all add variety and new dimensions of learning to the curriculum. Action songs and games have an appropriate time and place in the special class. For example, a group meets in a house provided by the church, and the opening of class takes place in the backyard with energetic songs and games. The group moves from lively songs to quieter ones till the class is sitting quietly, ready for the Bible story. The activity stirs the slow ones and tires the fast ones, besides oxygenating the brain in readiness for God's truth.

Remember to introduce one new idea at a time. Basically, you are there to teach the pupils of God's love and of their value and importance in His eyes.

Crafts utilizing touching, feeling, and doing—with textures and rich colors—are beneficial. Use full-color, true-to-life Bible pictures to illustrate the story. (No cartoons or caricatures; also no black and white line drawings. People with poor perception cannot assimilate such illustrations.)

Allow the pupils to participate in the story. Use their names often. Touch those nearest you. Be animated. Use emotion. Be close to the group. Identify and share from your own life. It's *"us,"* not *"them."*

Encourage pride of accomplishment. Some of the activities will be ongoing for the class—a mural or scrapbook or gifts for the parents on appropriate holidays. However, when possible, try to complete projects each Sunday.

The hyperactive child with a minute attention span should be taught on a one-to-one basis, away from the group. He may rejoin the class for crafts and music or playtime, but simply can't respond to the Bible story in the group. Take him to another room for the Bible lesson.

All of the students needs a quiet time, and so do you, Teacher! A snack may be served while the youngsters listen to a favorite record or two, or watch a filmstrip. A word about the juice and cookie routine: BEWARE. Your class registration sheet *must* list the students' allergies, aversions, and special diets. Most mentally disabled people have hidden physiological malfunctions which can include hypoglycemia. We know today that many food additives, as well as sugar, are dangerous to individuals. A wise procedure is to avoid sweets in all forms. Serve pure juices and raw fruits or vegetables. Check with the parents or guardians of your pupils, if such information has not been provided.

The classroom environment should be calm and consistent, but even in that context it can echo with music and laughter! The calm is a reflection of your confidence in Christ. And the consistency is proof of His faithfulness in answering prayer.

The word "flexibility" is still the key. Some Sundays the young people may want to sing more than on other Sundays. They may want to use the rhythm instruments or march in glad celebration! Other Sundays the craft may be more time-consuming. The idea is to be so well prepared that the schedule need not be adhered to rigidly.

Here is a word about toileting your charges. Determine who needs to be reminded, who needs help, and who is able to care completely for himself. This is one area that cannot be scheduled. Some youngsters need more liquid intake because of medication or because of their condition, while others may be on limited fluids. Make it your business to *know the individual needs.* You must also be aware of possible seizure activity. (See registration form.) As you learn to know your students, you will be able to detect subtle or overt behavior differences which reveal a change in, or a lack of medication. (If John is absolutely impossible to deal with, it's a safe guess that Mother forgot to give him his pill.)

Personnel in the Special Education Department

Special Education requires a large staff. Some of the youngsters may need a one-on-one teaching situation, and most will need help and supervision during the session.

A personnel roster and job description could look like the following:

1. *Director or supervisor of the entire Special Education program.*

   Advisor to all special classes, which can encompass Sunday School, Junior Church, deaf and blind ministries, club activities, day school, and recreation.

   Liason between classes

   Friend to parents—available for sharing and counseling

   Reports directly to the pastoral staff

   Provides teacher orientation

   Knows curriculums being used or needed

   Available to teaching staff for counsel and prayer

2. *Superintendent of Sunday School class*

   Responsible for teacher-student assignments

   Delegates the following aspects

   a. Music

   b. Crafts

   c. Bible lesson

   d. Orders curriculum

   e. Orients teachers to class

   f. Holds monthly staff meeting

   g. Attends departmental meeting with entire staff

   h. Prays for teachers and children

3. *Superintendent of second hour* (if included in your program)

   Responsible for teacher-student assignments

   Delegates aspects of class function

　　a. Music
　　b. Crafts
　　c. Bible lesson (often a review of Sunday School) or supervises attendance in the first part of the adult worship service
　　d. Supplies materials to teachers
　　e. Orients teachers to class
　　f. Holds monthly, weekly if needed, staff meeting
　　g. Attends departmental meeting with entire staff
　　h. Prays for teachers and children

4. *Secretaries for both hours,* (superintendent should assume role if no secretary).
Prepares rooms
Assigns activity centers
Takes roll
Keeps track of supplies
Registers visitors

5. *Teachers.* In summary, many of the teaching responsibilities have been mentioned in other chapters. They include:
To be present and prepared
To be "prayed up" and to have a clear conscience before God (1 John 1:9)
To be observant and sensitive to the unspoken needs of the students
To be a channel for God's love.
To notify superintendent of anticipated absence, ahead of time whenever possible
To be supportive of other staff and attend the meetings
To pray daily for the class members and their families
To be dependable, teachable, flexible

6. *Pastoral staff member*

Corrie ten Boom, well-known Christian writer, has a heartfelt ministry to the retarded. She knows that while the minds of these people do not function normally, their spirits respond wholly to the truth of Jesus Christ. Miss ten Boom implores her readers to tell the retarded about Jesus' love because they understand it very well. As Corrie's father told her years ago, "Corrie, what you do among these people is of little importance in the eyes of men, but I'm sure in God's eyes it is the most valuable work of all." [1]

Teacher, you are polishing God's jewels!

[1] Corrie ten Boom with C. C. Carlson, *In My Father's House* (Westwood, N. J.: Fleming H. Revell Co., 1976), p. 154.

6 The Church

—And the Childlike

The humbled human heart, obedient and dependent as a child, is valued by God.[1] Retarded people have these characteristics, which could serve as an example to the rest of us. However, these exact characteristics make the mentally retarded innocents such vulnerable prey in today's society. *It is the responsibility of the church to give them the Gospel of Jesus Christ to comfort them eternally, and God's standard to live by daily.*

The ministry should also serve the parents and families of the retarded by providing biblical supportive counseling, the opportunity to worship and to exercise their gifts within the body, and assistance with practical needs. Such a ministry may also provide current information about educational opportunities and medical facilities available within the community.)

Special Education enables the church to obey the scriptural mandate to bring children to Christ. Lay people within the fellowship of believers are perfectly capable of fulfilling this ministry through the power of the Holy Spirit. Men and women of all ages can have a place in special teaching. The ministry has proved to be beneficial for all involved, as well as for other members of the local congregation and the surrounding community.[2]

Your plan for Special Education can contain the following information:

Publicity: survey of community
1. Determine types of special education classes in public school in the area
2. Assess community resources:
   a. Park and recreation facilities
   b. YMCA and YWCA clubs
   c. Boys' and girls' clubs
   d. Special Girl or Boy Scout groups
   e. Regional center for mentally disabled
   f. Institutions or residential schools
3. Special classes in other churches
4. Dialogue with all the foregoing as well as finding and filing related newspaper or magazine coverage
5. Brochure produced by your church

Pupils: where are they?
1. Contact public and private special school PTA groups
2. Talk to parents of retarded in your church. They know others
3. Advertise, and distribute brochures
4. Announce intent to Regional Center, local National Association for Retarded Citizens, public and private clinics, and facilities listed in the yellow pages of your telephone directory

Personnel: recruiting and commitment
1. Exciting and challenging appeal to congregation
2. Orientation sessions
   a. Audiovisual presentation
   b. Dialogue with other teachers
   c. Parental input
   d. Observation of operative classes
   e. Discussion and planning of your particular special education program
3. Individual pastoral interview for each teacher
4. Discussion with church's Director of Special Education
5. Delegation of responsibility

Program: what do we do when we get together?
1. Determination of time and place
2. Curriculum: Scripture Press Special Education Bible Curriculum
3. Reinforcement and correlation of each concept in a variety of ways allowing the best use of time.

Prayer—involvement and support of the program by:
1. Leadership nucleus and governing body
2. Pastoral staff
3. Congregation
4. Special Education staff
5. Parents

Even an established class for the retarded requires continuing support by the congregation. Some churches report that their ministry to the retarded has been adopted by a specific group within the assembly. In one instance, an adult Sunday School pledged prayer and practical help. They maintained the facility, provided specific needs, took the entire group on outings, and supported various projects such as the Christmas play and party.

A sharing Special Education staff creates an aware and caring congregation. This, in turn, lightens the parental burden. Remember, people cannot respond with love to those they do not know. Every child and adult within the assembly should be familiar with the dear, different ones in their midst. The assurance of this welcome and love for the *entire* family does more to attract those outside the fold than mere lip service or pity. This is Christianity in action! This is Koinonia!

Your functioning Special Education class provides unlimited horizons and vision!

When It's Not Sunday

There are many social opportunities within the church which can encourage integration and mutual appreciation. Whenever possible, the retarded people should be included in musical presentations, holiday celebrations, dinners, group entertainments and special services. Also, if and as youngsters improve, they may be woven into the main fabric of the regular Sunday classes.

Weekday clubs provide another opportunity to expand your ministry. Most churches that meet on Wednesday evenings have club programs for the young people. A New Jersey church has established a Pioneer Girls group for retarded girls. They are known as "The Shepherds," and work under the auspices of the church's regular Pioneer Girls' Committee. Whenever possible, youngsters should be integrated into the regular clubs, thus benefiting all concerned. However, a large enrollment of retarded individuals will necessitate separate clubs. The Special Education department in the church can also be of help to its counterpart in the public school system. Teachers, parents, and Sunday School personnel can pool their observations and experiences to the best advantage of the students in both Sunday School and public school.

A class for the retarded can give your congregation an outreach that may eventually include ministries to the physically disabled, the deaf, and the blind. The Good News of Jesus Christ should be readily available to every person!

Realistic goals bring your vision for the future into the reach of today.

Pray a class for retarded people into reality in your church! And be ready to catch the vision God wants implanted among the personnel. It won't end with just a Sunday School class!

This ministry is accompanied by specific and very special rewards. Special Education is a difficult and demanding area of service, but you will receive far more than you will give when you become a member of the team.

God made these children of His different, and we call them "special." But remember, "special" means "precious."

Precious jewels are valuable and require constant care and protection. Their loss or misplacement causes anguish to the owner.

Begin to gather and care for the precious, "special" ones right now! They are all around you.

The Owner has lovingly committed them to your supervision and care—for a while!

---

[1] Matthew 8:2-3.
[2] Matthew 5:14-16.

Epilogue and Reading List

Now that you have looked at the retarded with new eyes, and may be prepared to love and minister to them, you may want to do some further reading. The following may be of interest and assistance:

Carmichael, Amy. *IF*. Grand Rapids: Zondervan, 1965.

Craig, Eleanor. *P.S. Your Not Listening*. New York: Richard W. Baron Pub. Co., 1972.

Hong, Edna. *Bright Valley of Love*. Minneapolis: Augsburg Publishing House, 1976.

Powell, John, S.J. *Why Am I Afraid to Tell You Who I Am?* Chicago: Argus Communications (Peacock Books), 1969.

Stanford, Miles J. *Principles of Spiritual Growth*. Lincoln, Nebraska: Back to the Bible Radio Hour

Stubblefield, Harold. *The Churches' Ministry in Mental Retardation*. Nashville: Broadman, 1965.

As a teacher of the mentally retarded in Sunday School, you may bring a combination of gifts and talents to your students. But they also will contribute in ways which will enrich your time together.

Whatever your abilities, whatever their disabilities, always look for the treasure of eternal value that God has entrusted to your class!

You may have credentials that prove your eligibility to teach. You may have gathered knowledge from books. You may have a direct calling from God, or you may be searching for His will in this ministry.

My final word to all of you is to remember "the more excellent way" described by God in 1 Corinthians 13.

The most effective vehicle through which one touches the eternal souls of others, for the glory and honor of Jesus Christ, is His own love as the center of your life!